A GLOW-IN-THE-DARK STICKER FILE

ILLUMINATING FACTS
THE SKELETON

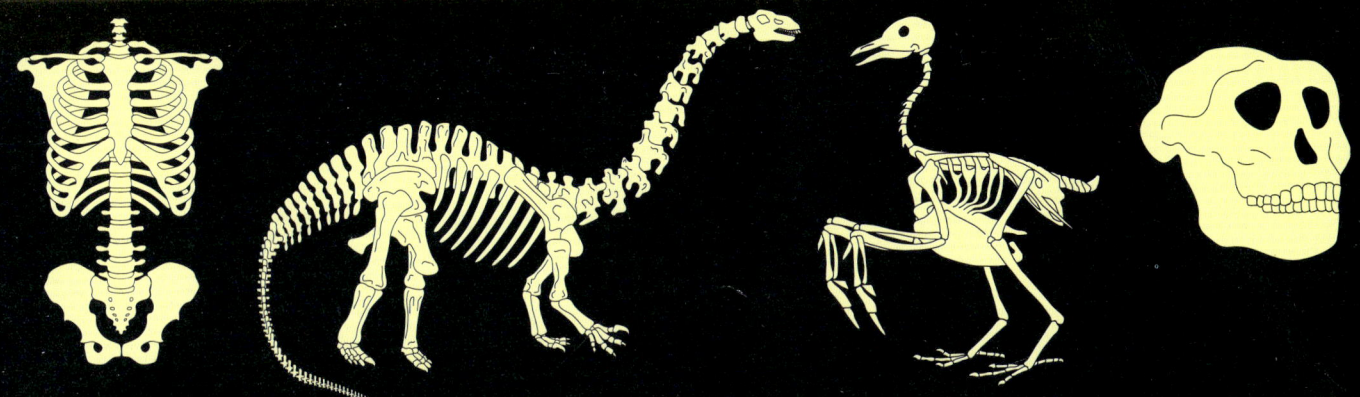

Mammals, reptiles and birds all have one thing in common – they all have some form of skeleton. This bony structure, powered by muscles, pulled by tendons and held together by joints and ligaments, is clothed in flesh and covered in skin. Over millions of years skeletons have evolved and developed to give humans and other creatures the appearance we recognise.

There are many fascinating facts to learn about skeletons. Fossils of prehistoric bones can show us how creatures would have looked millions of years ago. Comparing them with modern bones can show how much, or how little, the skeleton has changed – in fact, some living creatures have not changed much at all.

This glow-in-the-dark sticker file will help you to learn about skeletons. You can peel the stickers from the middle of the book and stick them on the special panels. If you take the book apart carefully you will find that the sticker panels make posters which you can hang on the walls of your room. To get the best glow, charge the stickers by exposing them to a good, bright light – then view them in total darkness.

Product Development for Red Bird by Martin Rhodes-Schofield
Written, Designed and Illustrated by Chapman Bounford and Associates
Special Effects, Reproduction and Print by Technographic Suffolk IP19 8TS England

© Red Bird Publishing 1999 Brightlingsea Colchester CO7 0SX England

DINOSAUR SKELETONS

Dinosaurs are perhaps the most familiar of all pre-historic creatures. They were similar to reptiles (dinosaur means 'terrible lizard') and lived throughout the world, slowly evolving over a period of 140 million years until they suddenly disappeared about 65 million years ago.

Although fossilised pre-historic bones had been discovered in the past it was only one hundred years or so ago that scientists began to make a thorough study of them. Palaeontology is the name we give to the study of extinct creatures.

Since the early days of the study many thousands of bones from almost as many different creatures have been found. These fossil bones are preserved in layers of rock. They are only discovered millions of years after the creatures died, when the rocks are cracked open – by natural forces, mining and quarrying, or by fossil hunters.

It is rare for a complete skeleton to be found but experts are able to work out what the creatures looked like from very few bone samples. Modern techniques are used by scientists to establish exactly how old bones are. They can tell what sort of foods an animal would eat by studying its teeth and they know from the limbs and joint structures how it would have moved and how quickly.

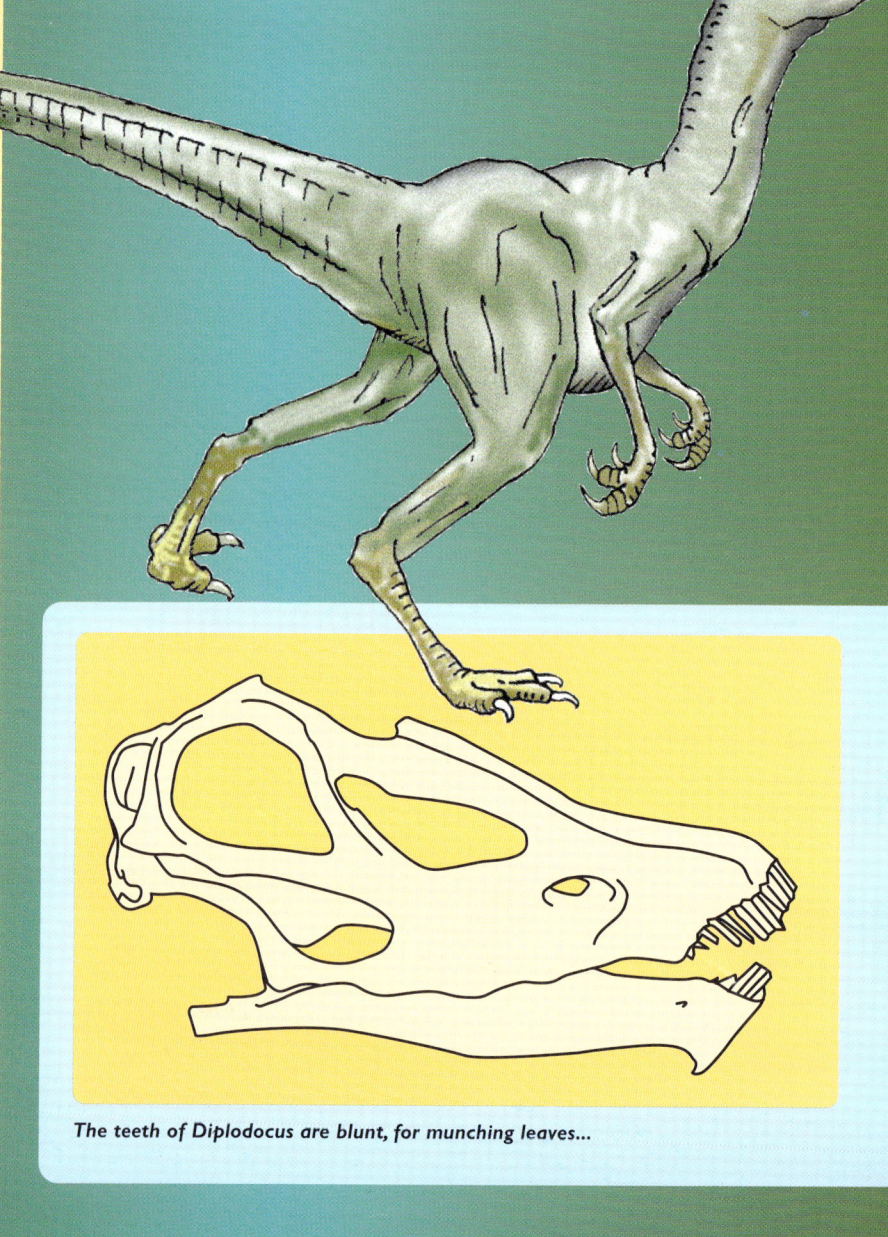

The teeth of Diplodocus are blunt, for munching leaves...

DINOSAUR SKELETONS

Sizes of different types of dinosaur varied greatly. Some were no bigger than a small dog. Others, like Apatosaurus (*below*), were huge, up to 23 metres (75 feet) long. They had specially adapted skeletons to allow them to lift their necks. The coelurid (*below left*) is much smaller, about two metres (six feet) long. Its sharp claws and teeth show that it was a hunter or scavenger. It could probably move extremely fast too.

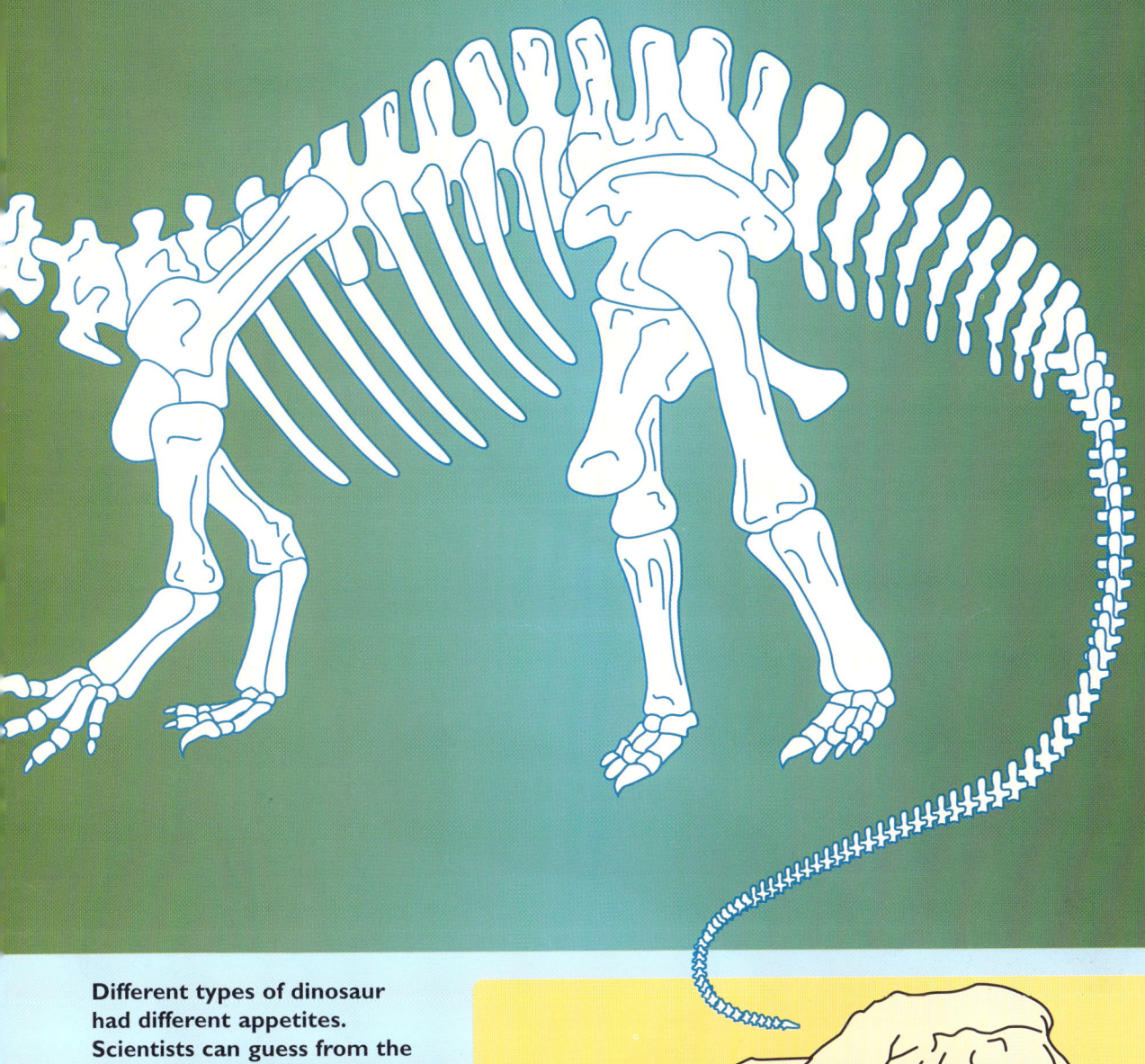

Different types of dinosaur had different appetites. Scientists can guess from the shape of teeth and from the general build of the creature whether it was a flesh-eating carnivore or a plant-eating herbivore. They can also see what type of vegetation would have existed at that time from other fossils discovered in the locality of the fossilised bones.

...in contrast, a carnivore would have sharp fangs for tearing through flesh.

DINOSAUR SKELETONS

GLOW-IN-THE-DARK STICKER PANEL

Dinosaurs developed in many different ways during the time they roamed the earth. Some could fly, like the Pterodactyl (1). The little Euparkeria (2) could run on just its hind legs. The long neck of the Apatosaurus (3) enabled it to eat leaves from trees. The Stegosaurus (4) had huge plates that stood up along its back. These were probably used to keep it cool. The Archaeopteryx (5) had feathers.

HUMAN EVOLUTION

The evidence from fossil bones found in various parts of the world shows that human beings evolved from earlier forms. Scientists believe that some other modern creatures – apes such as the chimpanzee and the gorilla – are closely related to humans. They probably share the same ancestry.

As with other pre-historic creatures, complete skeletons of early humans are rarely discovered. But scientists can discover a great deal about the appearance and probable behaviour of early humans from the few fossilised bones that are found and from other items found close by.

Skeleton reconstructions show that humans changed a lot during the long process of evolution to become the beings they are today.

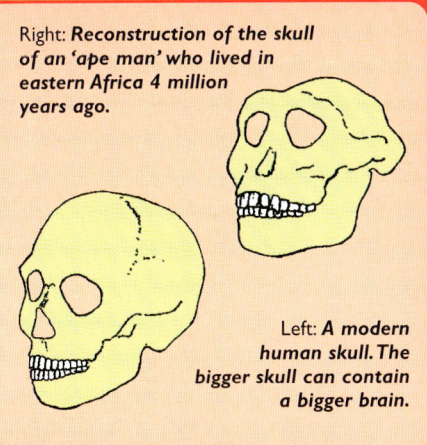

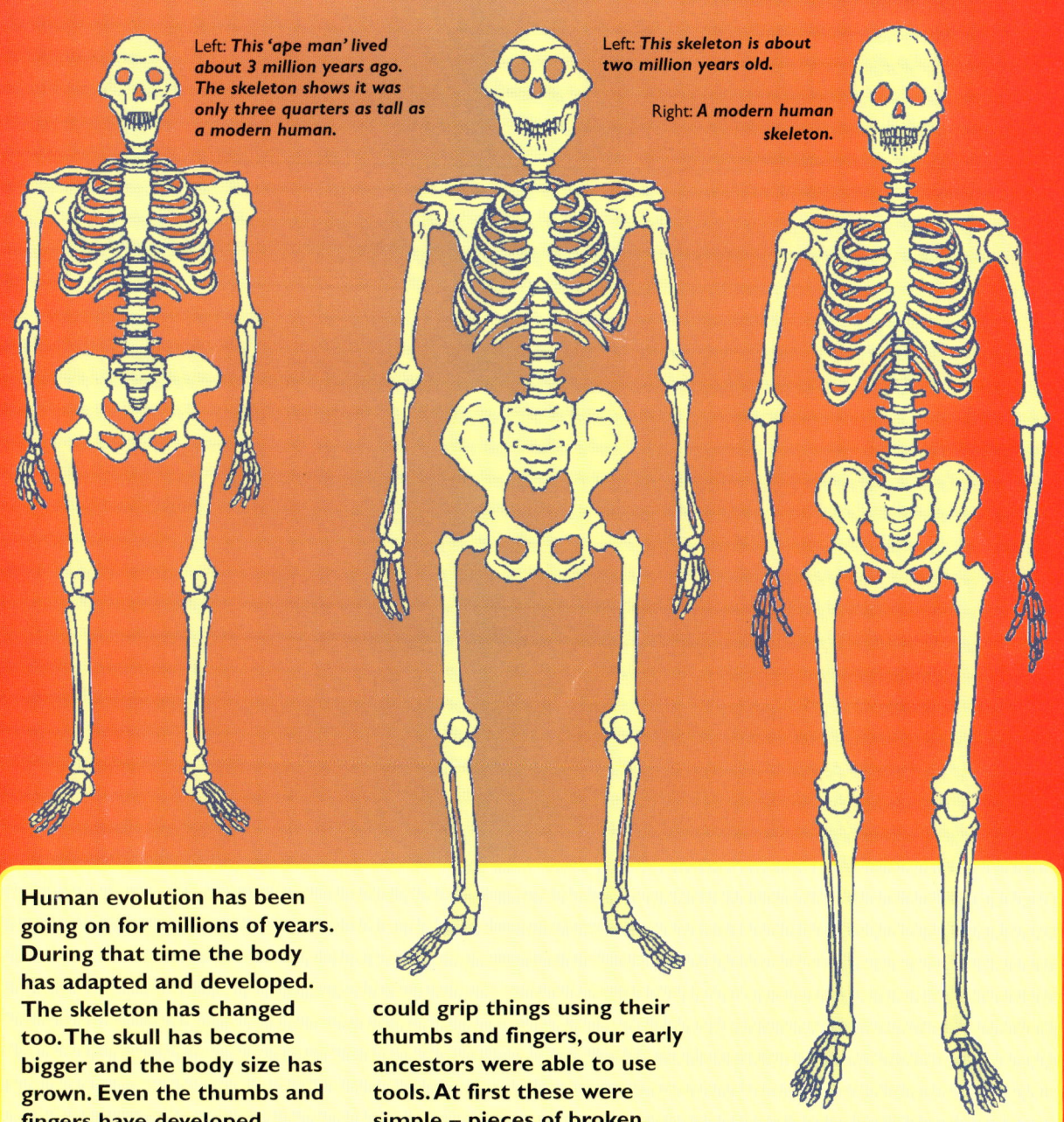

Right: *Reconstruction of the skull of an 'ape man' who lived in eastern Africa 4 million years ago.*

Left: *A modern human skull. The bigger skull can contain a bigger brain.*

Left: *This 'ape man' lived about 3 million years ago. The skeleton shows it was only three quarters as tall as a modern human.*

Left: *This skeleton is about two million years old.*

Right: *A modern human skeleton.*

Human evolution has been going on for millions of years. During that time the body has adapted and developed. The skeleton has changed too. The skull has become bigger and the body size has grown. Even the thumbs and fingers have developed.

In fact, the development of our hands has been crucial to our survival. Because they could grip things using their thumbs and fingers, our early ancestors were able to use tools. At first these were simple – pieces of broken rock or sticks. Basic tools like these were used for hunting. Nowadays we can use highly sophisticated tools. We can type on keyboards and play musical instruments.

HUMAN SKULL AND TEETH

The skull contains and protects the eyes and the brain. We usually think of the skull as one big dome-shaped bone with a moveable jaw. In fact it is made up of 29 bones. Most of these are firmly fixed together. Only the lower jaw bone and three tiny bones in each ear can move.

When babies are born some of the plates which make the skull are not rigidly joined. As the baby grows its brain grows and the skull can expand. It takes several years for the joints to harden and the skull to be fixed in its final shape.

There are tiny bones in the ear and these are moved by sound vibration. The movements are turned into signals that travel along nerves into the brain.

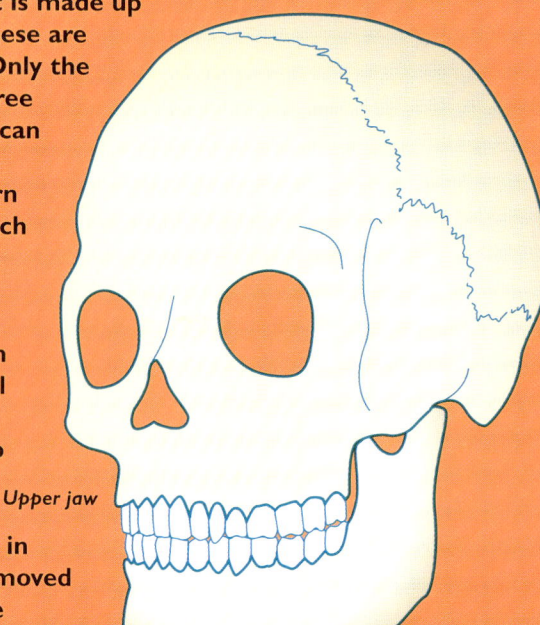

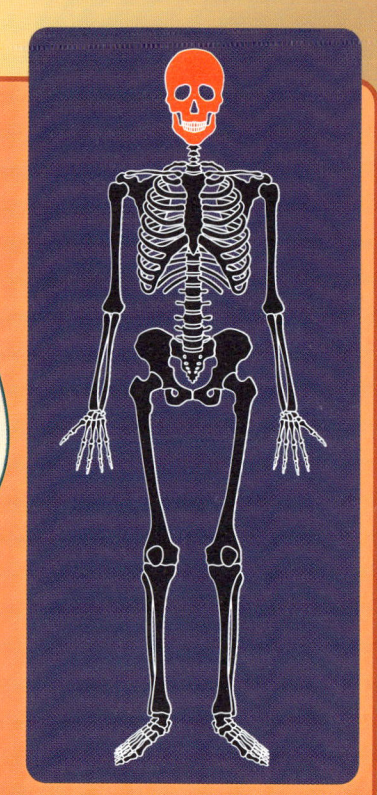

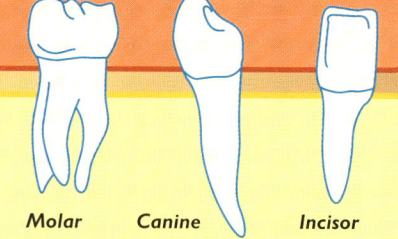

Upper jaw

Lower jaw

Molar *Canine* *Incisor*

Teeth are not bones, although they are very hard. They are attached to the skull, set in sockets in the upper and lower jaw.

There are three shapes of tooth, each with a different job. The incisors are wedge-shaped with a sharp edge and are at the front of the mouth. They cut food when we bite. Canines are pointed teeth, set next to the incisors. Canines grip and tear food.

Behind these teeth come the premolars and molars. They are square shaped with nobbles on. They grind the food up as we chew it.

Like bones, teeth are living things. They have a blood supply and nerves – which is why they hurt if they are damaged or diseased. Cleaning teeth regularly helps avoid tooth decay and disease.

Because children's mouths are small and their jaws will grow, we have two sets of teeth. The first teeth grow when we are young. We call these 'milk' teeth. By the time we are ten years old they will have been replaced with bigger, stronger adult teeth.

There are ten milk teeth in the upper jaw and ten in the lower jaw. there are sixteen adult teeth in each jaw.

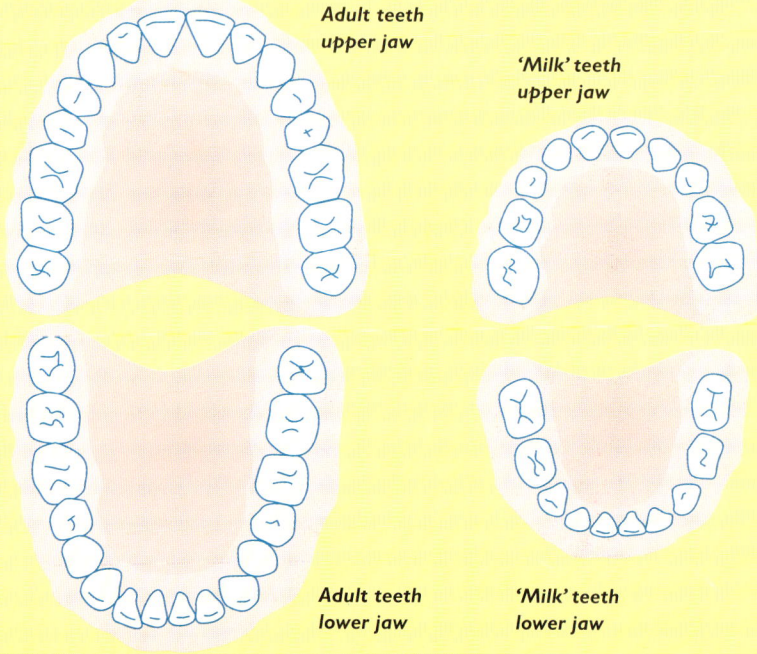

Adult teeth upper jaw

'Milk' teeth upper jaw

Adult teeth lower jaw

'Milk' teeth lower jaw

HUMAN SPINE, SHOULDERS AND RIBS

The rib bones form a cage which gives the shape to our chest. The cage contains and protects organs such as the heart and lungs. There are twelve ribs on each side of the body. Ribs are joined to the spine at the back and all but the lowest two on each side are fixed to a bone called the breastbone at the front.

You can easily feel your rib cage through your skin. The ribs move as we breathe, making the lungs expand and contract.

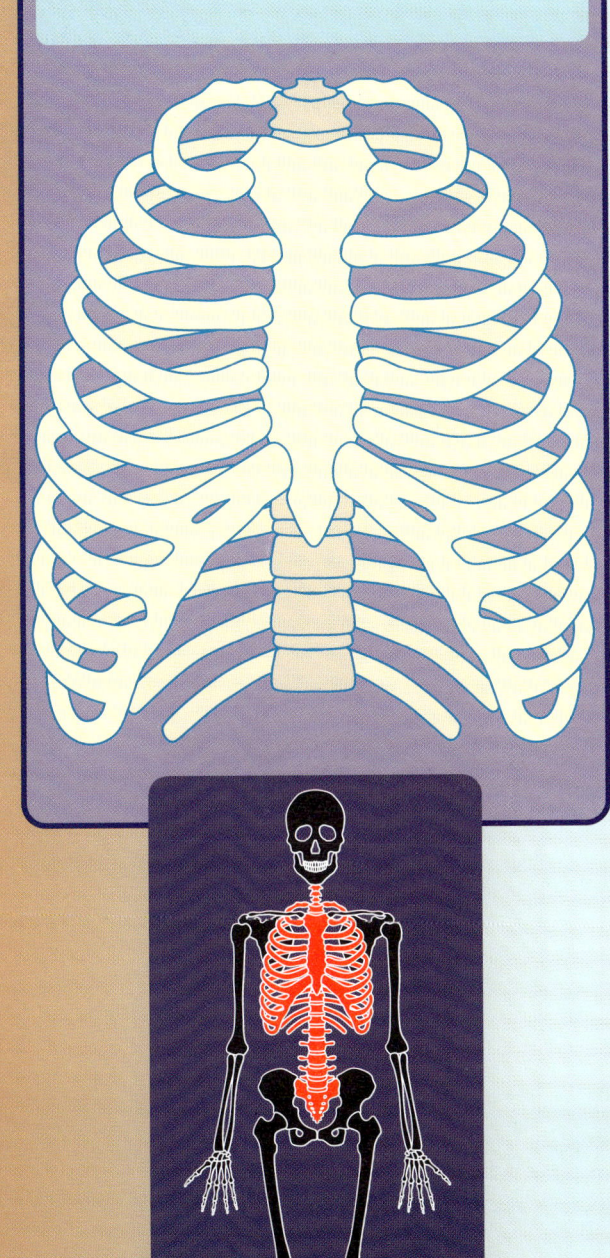

The spine looks like a tall, wobbly stack of 33 bones called vertebrae. It runs up the middle of our body. At the top is the skull. At the bottom the lowest nine bones are firmly joined together in two groups and fixed to the pelvis. Each of the other bones in the stack is separated from the one above and the one below it by a disk of flexible material called cartilage. The spine is very flexible, so we can bend backwards, forwards and from side to side. We can even twist our shoulders and hips.

A thick rope made of thousands of tiny nerve fibres runs through a channel in the spine. Like lots of electrical cables, these nerves connect all parts of the body with the brain. They carry the signals that take information to the brain and others that make our muscles move.

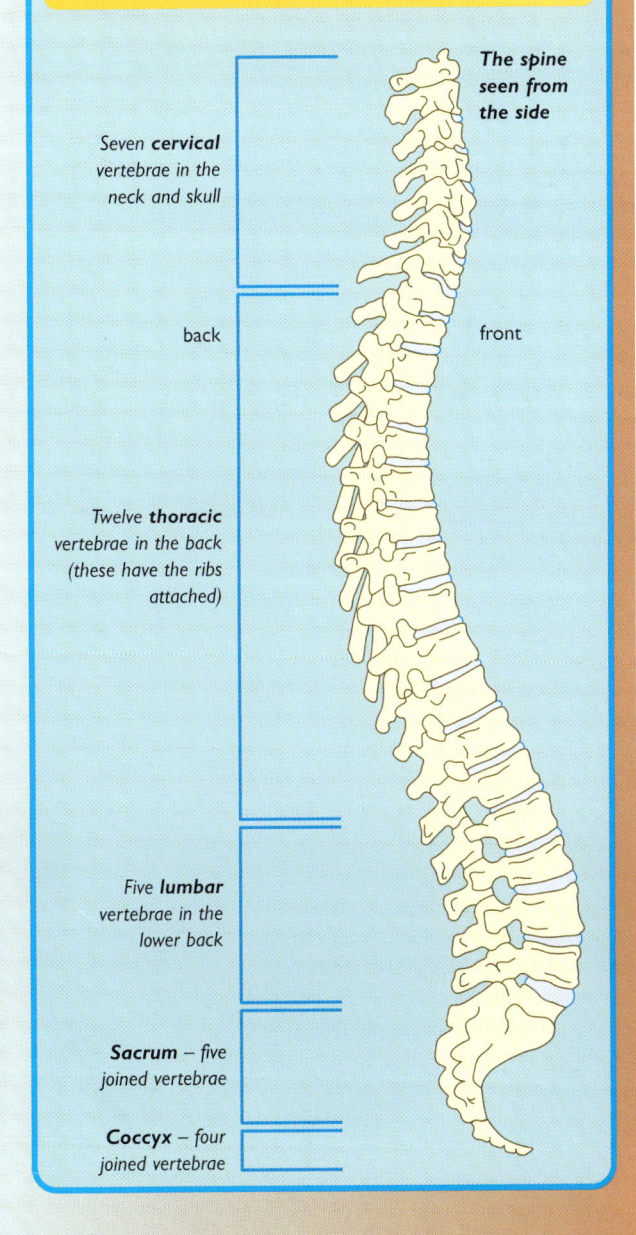

The spine seen from the side

back — front

Seven **cervical** vertebrae in the neck and skull

Twelve **thoracic** vertebrae in the back (these have the ribs attached)

Five **lumbar** vertebrae in the lower back

Sacrum – five joined vertebrae

Coccyx – four joined vertebrae

THE HUMAN SKELETON

GLOW-IN-THE-DARK STICKER PANEL

- Cranium
- Mandible
- Clavicle
- Humerus
- Vertebral column
- Ulna
- Radius
- Carpals
- Metacarpals

THE HUMAN SKELETON

GLOW-IN-THE-DARK STICKER PANEL

- Patella
- Fibula
- Metatarsals
- Tibia
- Tarsals
- Pelvis
- Femur
- Phalanges
- Phalanges

HUMAN SHOULDER, ARM AND HAND

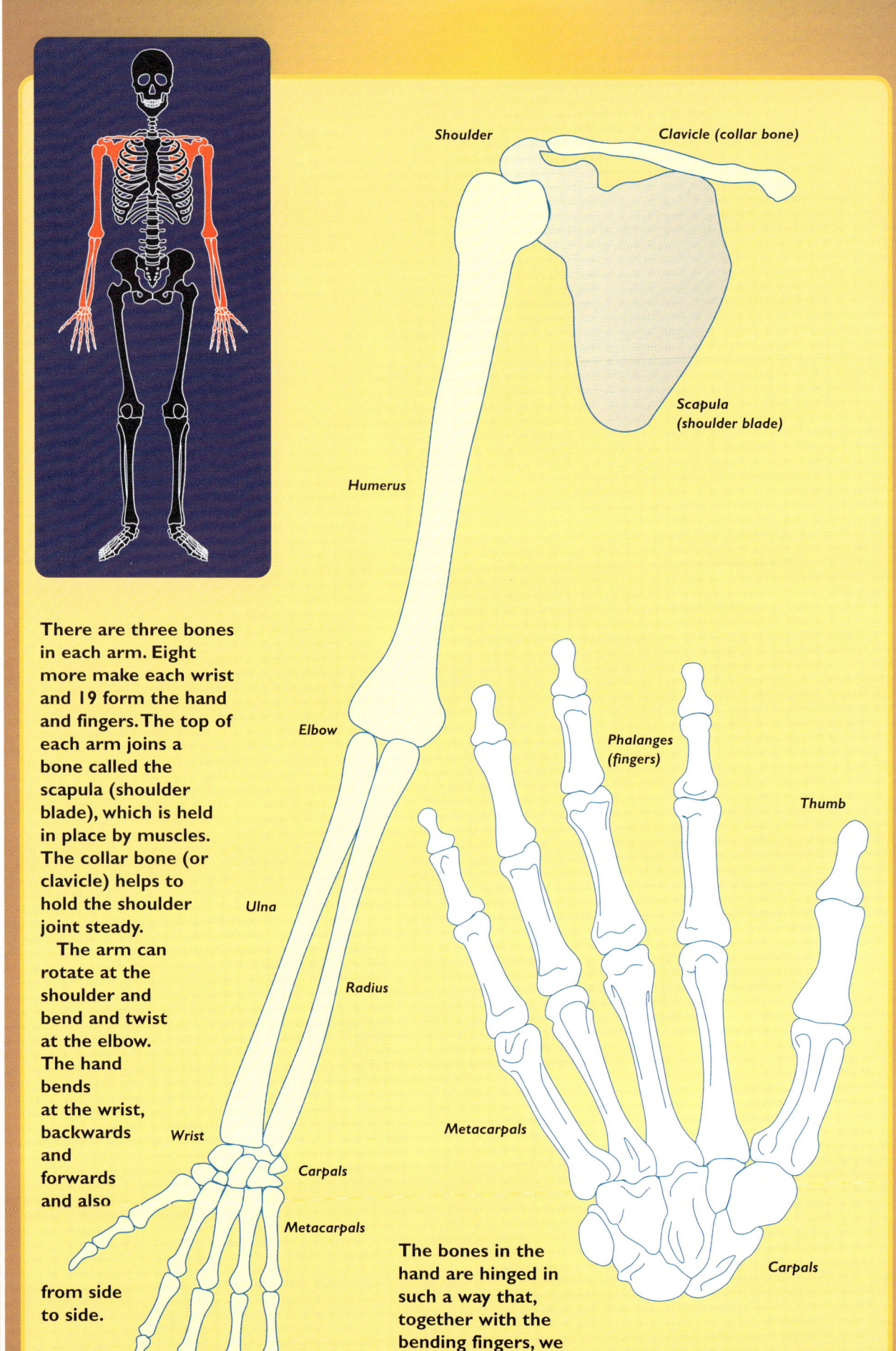

There are three bones in each arm. Eight more make each wrist and 19 form the hand and fingers. The top of each arm joins a bone called the scapula (shoulder blade), which is held in place by muscles. The collar bone (or clavicle) helps to hold the shoulder joint steady.

The arm can rotate at the shoulder and bend and twist at the elbow. The hand bends at the wrist, backwards and forwards and also from side to side.

The bones in the hand are hinged in such a way that, together with the bending fingers, we can grip objects.

Labels: Shoulder, Clavicle (collar bone), Scapula (shoulder blade), Humerus, Elbow, Ulna, Radius, Wrist, Carpals, Metacarpals, Phalanges, Phalanges (fingers), Thumb

HUMAN FOOT AND LEG

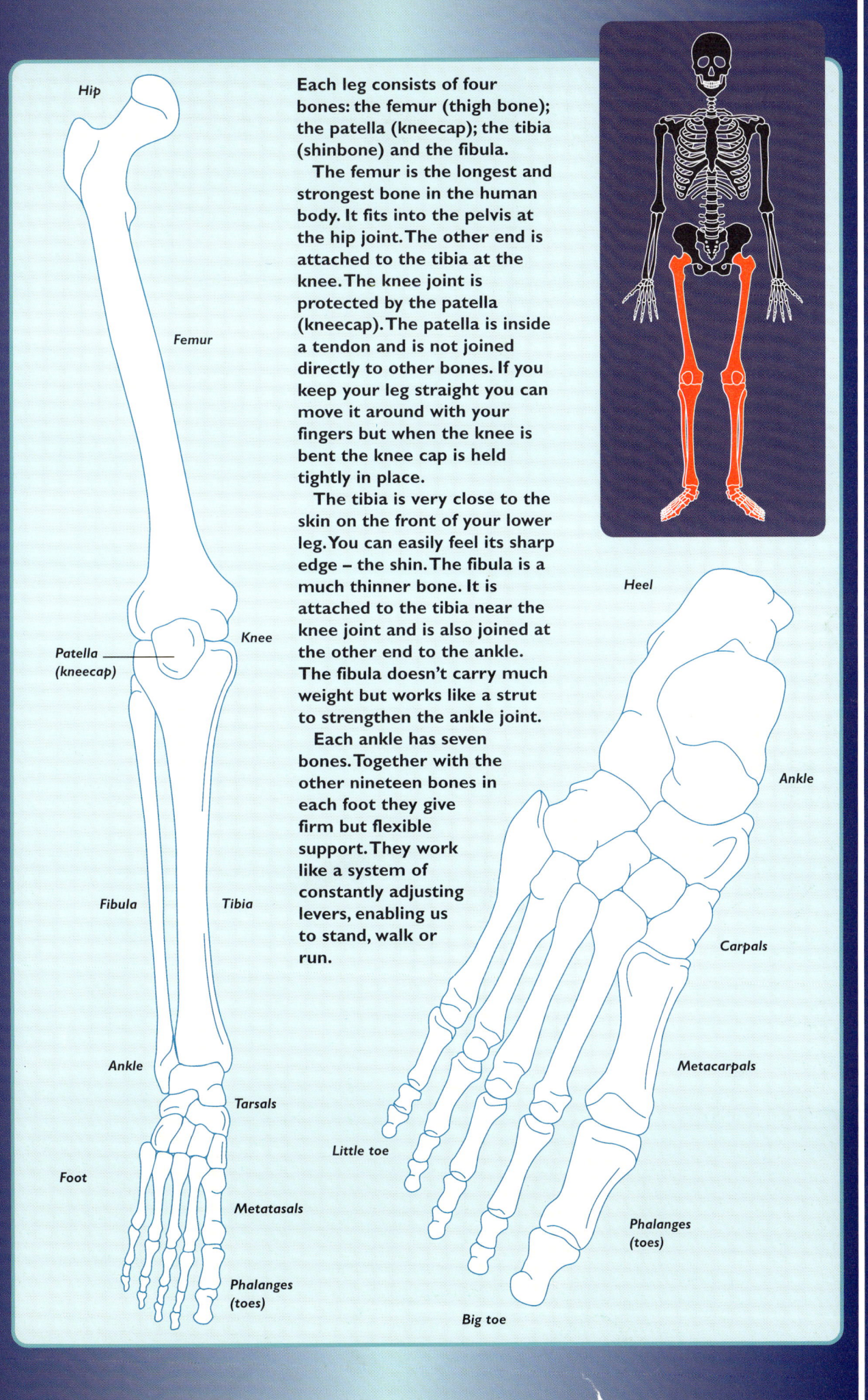

Each leg consists of four bones: the femur (thigh bone); the patella (kneecap); the tibia (shinbone) and the fibula.

The femur is the longest and strongest bone in the human body. It fits into the pelvis at the hip joint. The other end is attached to the tibia at the knee. The knee joint is protected by the patella (kneecap). The patella is inside a tendon and is not joined directly to other bones. If you keep your leg straight you can move it around with your fingers but when the knee is bent the knee cap is held tightly in place.

The tibia is very close to the skin on the front of your lower leg. You can easily feel its sharp edge – the shin. The fibula is a much thinner bone. It is attached to the tibia near the knee joint and is also joined at the other end to the ankle. The fibula doesn't carry much weight but works like a strut to strengthen the ankle joint.

Each ankle has seven bones. Together with the other nineteen bones in each foot they give firm but flexible support. They work like a system of constantly adjusting levers, enabling us to stand, walk or run.

HUMAN PELVIS, AND SKELETON GROWTH

The pelvic girdle is a ring of fused bones. The hipbones are actually made up of three bones – the ilium, the ischium and pubis. In children these bones are separate, and only join in early adolescence. The sacrum of the spine is joined to the hipbones.

The girdle surrounds a wide opening. In females the opening is wider than in males. This is because babies develop in the womb which is supported by the pelvic girdle and then they pass through the opening at birth. The shape of the pubic arch at the front of the girdle is also different.

On either side of the pelvis are the sockets where the ends of the thigh bones fit.

Hip bone

Female pelvic girdle

Sacrum

Coccyx

Pubic arch

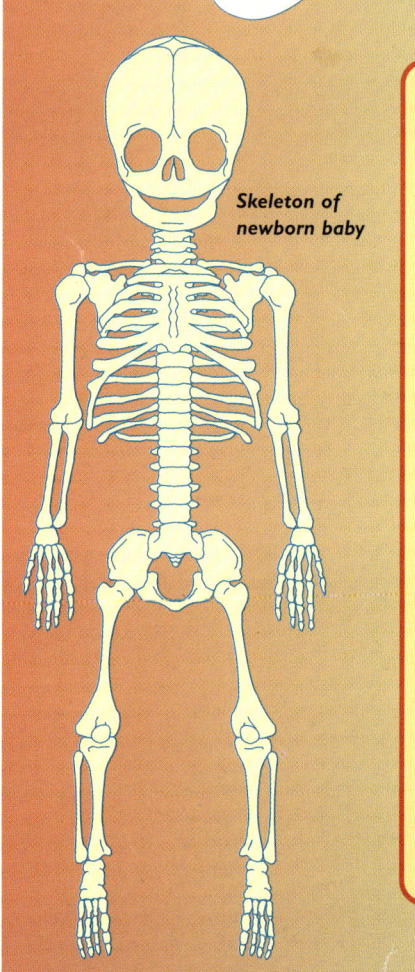

Male pelvic girdle

Skeleton of newborn baby

The human skeleton takes many years to develop to its adult form. A baby's skeleton has more individual bones than an adult, because many of the bones have not yet fused together. For example, a baby's skull consists of five bones joined by soft material. This allows the skull to grow as the brain grows, even though the baby's brain and skull are already large in proportion to its body.

Other proportions of the baby and adult skeletons are different. The baby's neck is shorter and its shoulders are higher. Its legs are also much shorter. As the legs grow, their shape changes, too.

The front of the baby's rib cage is rounded and will flatten as the child grows.

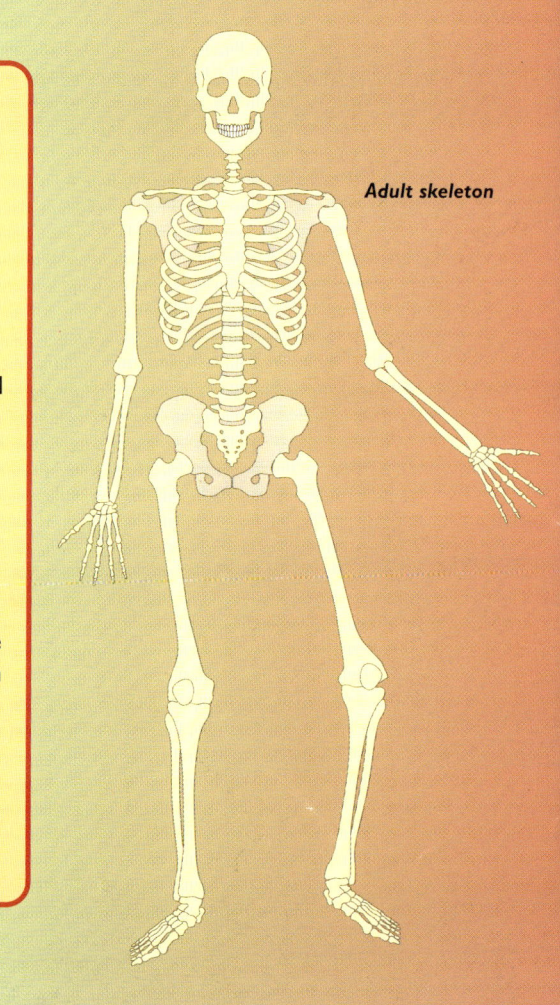

Adult skeleton

EVOLUTION OF SKELETONS

GLOW-IN-THE DARK STICKER PANEL

Above: The human being's nearest relative in the animal world may be the chimpanzee, but the skull of the human is shaped to hold a much larger brain than the chimp.

Below: The skeleton of a modern bird is remarkably similar to that of some dinosaurs. This shows how little some things change despite millions of years of evolution.

Below: The shape of a modern gorilla might give us an idea of how the human being's ancestors looked before they developed an upright walking posture.

Above: Over millions of years the human skull has slowly changed in shape. The brain cavity has increased in size as bigger brains have developed.

1. Dryopithecus — 18 million years ago
2. Australopithecus africanus — 5 million years ago
3. Homo erectus — 1 million years ago
4. Homo sapiens — 300,000 years ago
5. Homo sapiens sapiens — present day

RELATIVES OF HUMANS

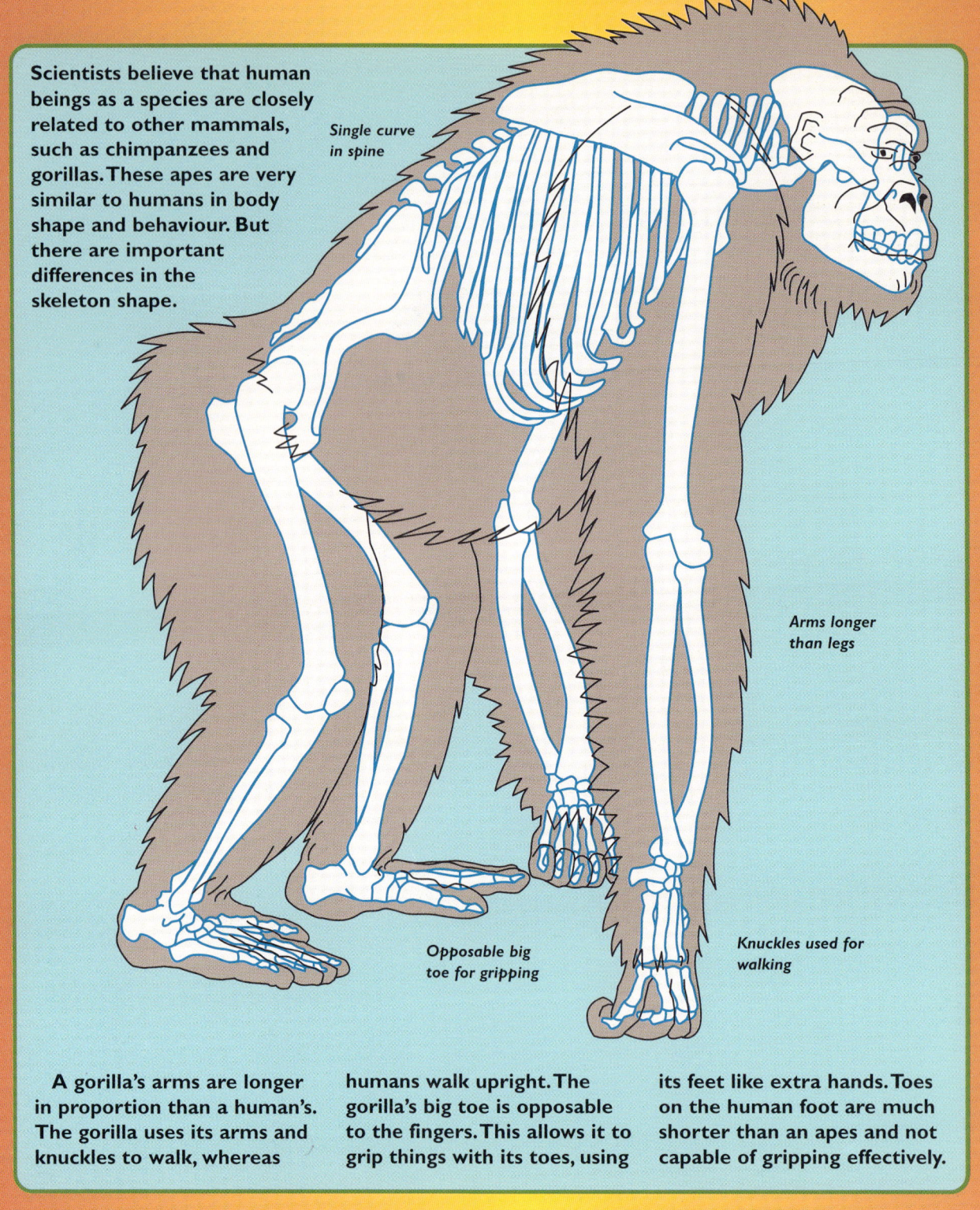

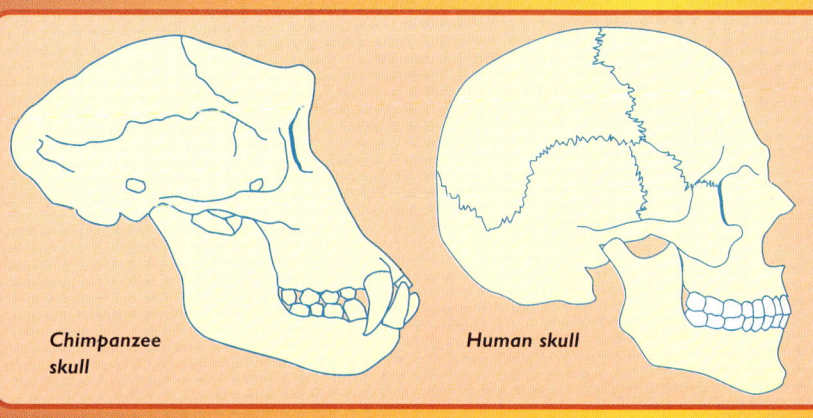

Scientists believe that human beings as a species are closely related to other mammals, such as chimpanzees and gorillas. These apes are very similar to humans in body shape and behaviour. But there are important differences in the skeleton shape.

Single curve in spine

Arms longer than legs

Opposable big toe for gripping

Knuckles used for walking

A gorilla's arms are longer in proportion than a human's. The gorilla uses its arms and knuckles to walk, whereas humans walk upright. The gorilla's big toe is opposable to the fingers. This allows it to grip things with its toes, using its feet like extra hands. Toes on the human foot are much shorter than an apes and not capable of gripping effectively.

Chimpanzee skull

Human skull

The large dome shape of the human skull holds a bigger brain than the skull of the chimpanzee.

RELATIVES OF HUMANS

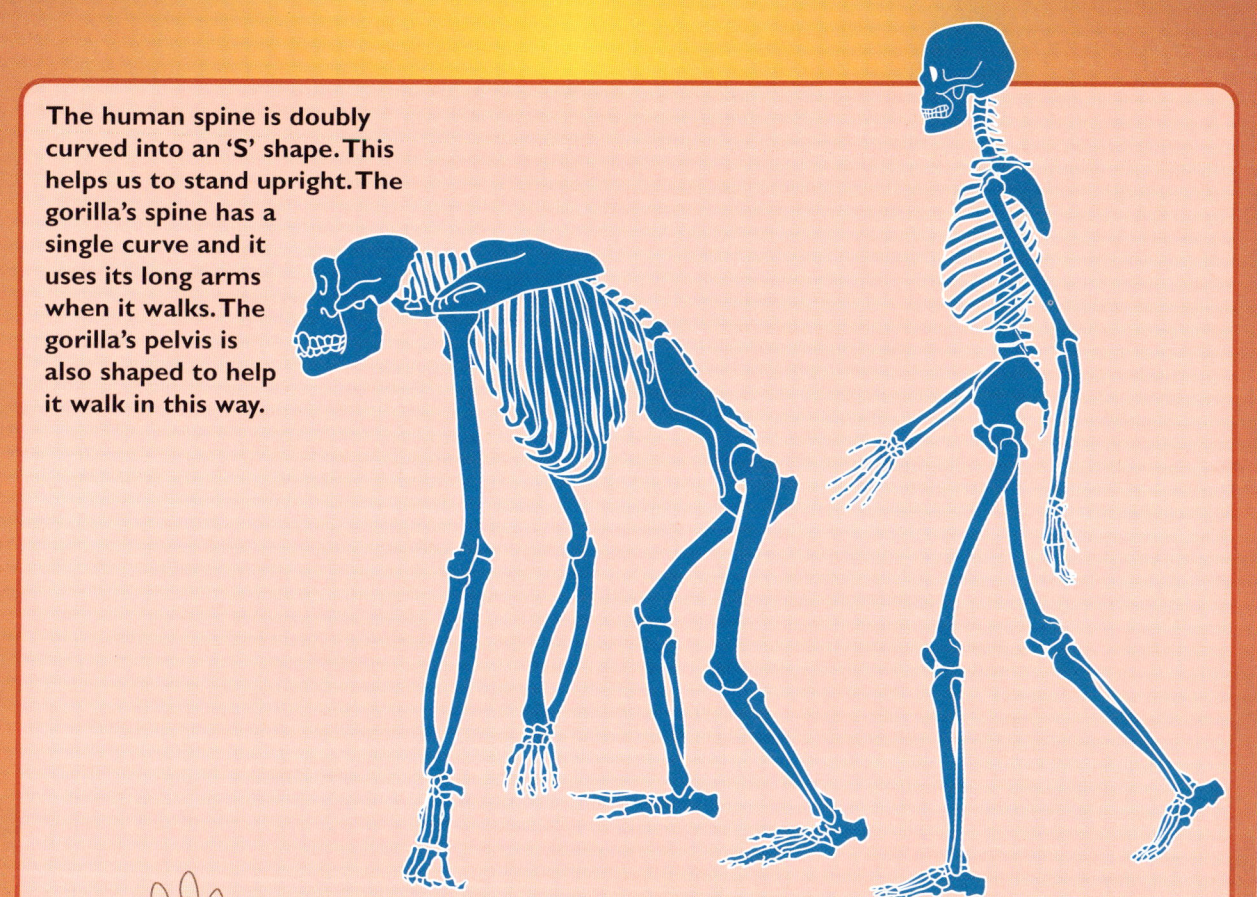

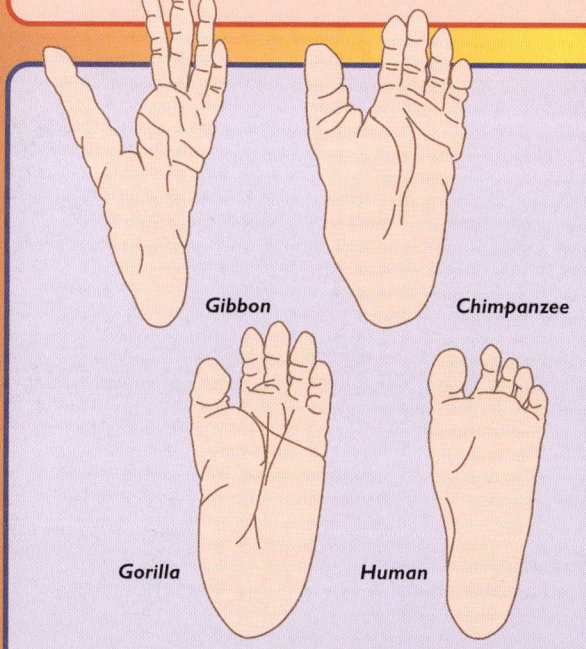

The human spine is doubly curved into an 'S' shape. This helps us to stand upright. The gorilla's spine has a single curve and it uses its long arms when it walks. The gorilla's pelvis is also shaped to help it walk in this way.

Gibbon *Chimpanzee*

Gorilla *Human*

Here we see the foot shape of humans next to those of three different apes. The gibbon has a very long big toe, very like a thumb, and uses its feet like another pair of hands to swing from branches of trees. The feet of chimpanzees and gorillas are more similar those of humans, but they have still have opposable big toes and retain the ability to grip. With its shorter, more or less parallel toes, the human foot is developed for walking rather than gripping.

The pelvis and lower limbs of humans differ in important ways from those of apes. The chimpanzee has a long pelvis and knees which are angled outwards which means that when it is walking bipedally (on two feet) it walks with a side-to-side rocking motion. Humans have upright leg bones with strong forward-pointing knees and flat feet, giving a smooth, upright walk.

LIVING PRE-HISTORY

Evolution has changed many of the creatures we see today so much that it is sometimes hard to recognise their early predecessors. Many other creatures have changed very little.

Today's crocodiles and alligators are very similar to early crocodilians that thrived 150 million years ago. In fact the main difference is size.

At four metres the modern crocodile is only one third of the size of one type of early crocodile, which almost certainly ate other dinosaurs.

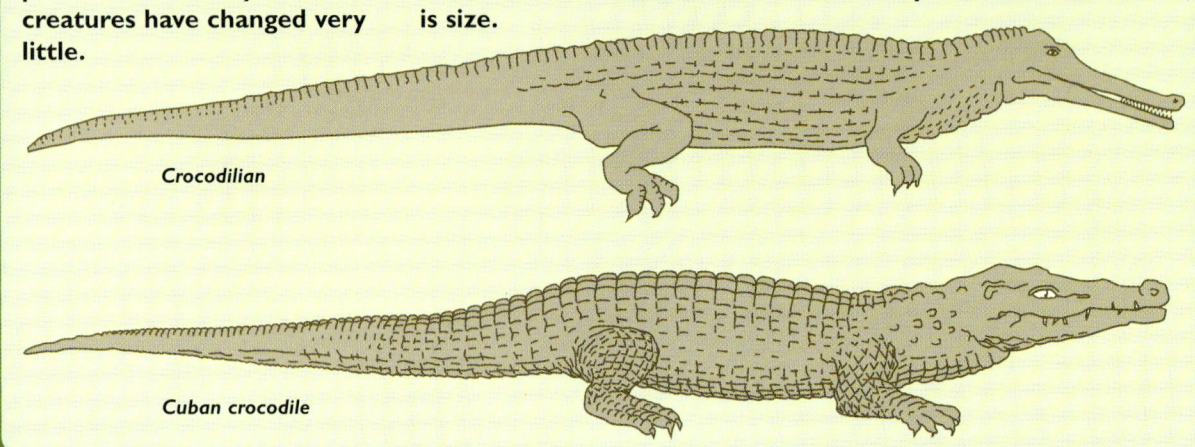

Crocodilian

Cuban crocodile

Perhaps surprisingly, one of the closest relatives of the dinosaur amongst modern creatures is the bird. Like crocodiles, bird skeletons have not changed much over millions of years. The picture on the right shows Archaeopteryx, an early bird-shaped creature, about one metre high, that lived 200 million years ago. Although its skeleton is very similar to that of several other types of dinosaur, the impressions of feathers in the fossil remains indicate that Archaeopteryx might have been capable of flying.

Archaeopteryx

Scientists are not certain whether Archaeopteryx could fly properly, or only glide. It might have used the claws on the front edge of its wings to help it climb trees in search of prey. Then it could glide down to the ground again.

Skeleton of a modern day bird

The skeleton of a modern bird is similar in some ways to the skeleton of Archaeopteryx, but also resembles those of other dinosaurs, too.